SUDDEN CHANGE

THE MEMOIR

CANDIA J. OLIVER

This is a work of nonfiction. Some names, identifying details, and events have been changed to protect the privacy of individuals.

First Edition

ISBN: 979-8-218-63053-9

Published by BYD CoCo Press

Printed in the United States of America

For inquiries, permissions, or rights requests, contact: press@bydcoco.com

I dedicate this book to my beloved niece Brit, who passed on March 28, 2005; my dear CJ, who passed on October 9, 2015; my brother O, who passed on May 6, 2013; my father Sol, who passed on March 3, 2018; and my stepmom Bunny, who passed away on February 21, 2024.

CJ, my dog, was a source of comfort and strength for Brit during her battle with Cancer, the "C" word, and I find peace knowing they are together now, embraced by God's love.

I also dedicate this to the many beautiful family members who have passed on yet remain close to my heart. To my grandmothers, Grandma Matti, who passed on January 6, 2006, and Nanny Melvena, who passed on July 25, 2012; to my grandfathers; and to my aunts, uncles, and cousins—your love and legacy continue to guide me every day.

AUTHOR'S NOTE

Life is a journey, and along the way there will be sudden changes—so you'd better buckle up. This book shares my personal journey and highlights how these changes can happen in the blink of an eye. While trials and tribulations are inevitable, they don't have to define us.

My journey has been both a psychological and emotional process. By letting go and letting God, I learned to connect with my authentic self. Surrendering my will to Him brought me clarity and strength, and it's my hope to show how I navigated that path and emerged stronger.

This book also sheds light on the importance and challenges of the "coming out phase" for lesbian, gay, bisexual, transgender, and queer individuals. Without proper support from family, friends, and society, this experience can feel isolating—or even devastating.

It's vital to recognize that LGBTQ+ individuals are as diverse as heterosexual individuals, with each person having their own unique identity and experiences. This book aims to uncover and celebrate the lives of LGBTQ+ people, highlighting their individuality and affirming their right to respect, understanding, and acceptance.

1

CHERRY HILL BEGINNINGS

I am Candia J. Oliver, and my parents are Joyce Lay-Moore and Solomon Oliver. My father, Sol, was short, dark-skinned, and handsome. Unfortunately, my father passed away in 2018. My mother and father separated after I was born. I grew up in Cherry Hill with my mother, three siblings, my mother's boyfriend, Roc, who was tall, light-skinned, and handsome--but passed away in 2017, and our dog, Victor, at 907 Cherry Hill Rd. I still love Cherry Hill. That is where my roots started.

Cherry Hill is home to Baltimore's largest public housing project—Cherry Hill Homes, which includes over 1,000 units, private homes, and several other low-income apartments throughout the community. Cherry Hill has various schools throughout the community: #164 Arundel Elementary, #159 Cherry Hill Elementary, #163 Patapsco Elementary, and #181 Southside Academy High, which was called #180 High School when I lived there. I attended #164 Arundel Elementary, where all of my teachers were wonderful. I attended Carver Vocational-Technical High School and majored in Business and Data Processing. I can still recall all my elementary, middle, and high school teachers. Cherry Hill is often seen as the worst place to live due to crime and drugs. However, I have a different opinion about the Cherry Hill community.

There are various things you can do in Cherry Hill. All of your necessities are right there for you, such as the supermarket, medical centers, recreation centers, the multi-purpose center where our library was located, and the community building where various activities were held. There are also parks—Reedbird and Middle Branch Park—and pools, including the Cherry Hill Aquatic Center which was called (the indoor) and the Cherry Hill Splash Park which was called (the outdoor).

We had various churches on every corner in Cherry Hill. I was a member of the United Methodist Church with my grandma Mate, which was right in the back of my house. My father's side of the family attended Community Baptist Church, and in our neighborhood there was also Cherry Hill Community Presbyterian, Christ Temple Apostolic Church, St. Veronica Catholic Church, and First Baptist Church. I used to go to church on Sundays with my maternal grandmother, and she had me baptized as a Methodist when I was a little girl. I was baptized again as a Christian in 2006; overall, I have a relationship with God, that is the way I see it. On January 27, 2018, I was baptized once more at Morning Star Baptist Church, which remains my church home to this day.

At the age of 5yrs old and in my elementary school years, my mother's boyfriend, Roc, my siblings and I had a special bond; we used to call him daddy. I loved him as a father, but I also knew who my biological father was, and my mother always reassured me of that. My mother was pregnant by Roc with twins but lost them. I remember that day so clearly because my oldest brother, Saul, helped get me dressed for kindergarten picture day. My mother left the dress out that she wanted me to wear, but, of course, Saul dressed me in another outfit. He really called himself styling me, and I must say—he did a great job because I looked adorable. I still have that picture today!

Roc took great care of my mother, siblings, and me. My mother and Roc decided to get a dog because they were tired of people breaking into our house. We named him Victor, a German Shepherd who all of the police officers in our area wanted to be their Police K-9. I tell you, Victor protected us, and we loved him so much! Unfortunately, he died from eating too much table food when I was in the 4th grade in 1975, and it hurt us so much. My mother and Roc didn't always have enough money to buy Victor dog food. Victor was buried in the woods by the Multi-Purpose Building in Cherry Hill. The building isn't there anymore, but another building has been built on the same land. When my mother and Roc, unfortunately, parted ways, he would still pick me up and bring me around his family and friends' houses.

Family isn't always about blood—it's about the people who show up for you, love you, and make you feel safe. Some of the most important people in my life became family through the bonds we built. And that's exactly how I gained my godmother, Lauren.

My godmother, Lauren, is brown-skinned, medium height, pretty, and always made me feel safe. I'll never forget the day I asked her to be my godmother.

We were at Hecht's Department Store on Howard Street, riding opposite escalators—Lauren on one side, me on the other. I couldn't hold it in, so I yelled across to her,

"Can you be my godmother?"

Without hesitation, she yelled back,

"Yes, Candy."

3

I was overjoyed! As soon as we reached the bottom of the escalators, we ran to each other and hugged tight. That moment meant everything to me—it sealed a bond that would last a lifetime.

I spent so much time at Lauren's house—at least twice a week and most weekends. And if I wasn't there, I was calling her on the phone. If Lauren wasn't home, her mother, Ms. Annta, had her own way of making sure my calls were heard.

She would shout right out the window and down the street,

"Lauren! Candy on the phone!"

Lauren, from wherever she was, would respond,

"Tell her I'll call her back."

But Ms. Annta wasn't having that. She'd shout back,

"Lauren Annta! Come and get this phone right now!"

Those moments are etched in my heart because they weren't just about phone calls—they were about family, love, and the joy of being truly connected.

It was the fall of 1977, and it was time to return to school from summer break. I was 11 years old, going to the 5th grade, and I met Doris in the 3rd grade, but developed a close friendship with her in the 5th grade—and we are still best friends today. Doris was dark-skinned, with long ponytails, and taller than me. I had seen Doris around, but never played with her until we were in the same class together.

I will never forget when we had to line up on the school playground on the first day of school, and Mr. Max called our names from his list of the children in his class. Mr. Max called my name first, and I began crying; then he called Doris' name, which triggered her to cry, too. We both cried because there was a rumor around the school that Mr. Max was mean and would fail students quickly. The thought frightened me because I had already repeated the 3rd grade before.

My 3rd-grade teacher, Ms. Brone, said, "She failed me because I talked too much," although I completed all of my work. Consequently, I feared Mr. Max because I always loved to talk and had the reputation of being a class clown. Mind you, I always did my schoolwork and did an excellent job at it!

Once we were in class, Doris and I talked about how much we wished we were not in Mr. Max's class. I had a revelation that Mr. Max was not as bad as people claimed he was. Actually, I really enjoyed him and learned a lot from him. Mr. Max made me realize that it is better to have a stern teacher that can really help you learn than a passive teacher that is going to allow you to do whatever you want. I was the type of student that definitely needed a stern teacher. If I could sense that I could bogart a class, that teacher better watch out—because it was on!

Doris was pretty much the sneaky, quiet type in school. We hit it off well; weeks passed as Doris and I became friends. When we returned home from school, we would do our homework and then meet outside to play.

Doris lived around the corner from me, and we started going over to each other's houses, which is where I met her parents. Mr. Frank and Mrs. Wilkins were both very nice. Unfortunately, they both passed away later in our adulthood. I had become very close with both of her parents—especially Mrs. Wilkins; I actually considered her my second mother. She considered me her daughter, as well. I could talk to Mrs. Wilkins about anything and everything, even when Doris upset me.

As our friendship progressed, Doris and I grew closer. She became a special person in my life and still is today. We dressed alike, and just did everything friends would do together. We went to the movies, played baseball, and swam together. I played football with the boys, but Doris did not.

Instead of coming home from school and meeting to play outside, I would go straight over to Doris' house after finishing my homework. Doris would make us tuna fish sandwiches, and we would drink Pepsi. I began staying at her house frequently, and we used to have so much fun together.

Doris and I would get upset with each other if we were around any other friends. She began hanging around two friends, Patsy and Nutty, whom I could not stand for her to be around. I used to think they were trying to pull her away from me, and that would bother me so much. When Doris and I had plans to go somewhere, Patsy and Nutty would talk her out of going with me. I would talk to Mrs. Wilkins about how I felt about Patsy and Nutty. Mrs. Wilkins would say, "It's all right for Doris to have other friends!" She did not see what I was seeing in the friends Doris associated with. Doris and I reassured each other that we were best friends. We began feeling more comfortable with our friendship, so we started branching out and being around other people.

My mother is petite, with light skin and long, pretty, black, wavy, thick hair. Absolutely beautiful. When I say beautiful, I mean looks, heart, mind, body, soul, and spirit. Despite how beautiful and amazing my mom is, major life changes occurred once my mom met a man named Jim, whom she eventually married! Jim was tall, dark-skinned, and not too good looking at all. He appeared nice and quiet when my mother introduced my siblings and me to him. My oldest brother, Saul, and oldest sister, Nelly, did not like him immediately. I don't know what they saw, but they did not like him. My middle brother, Daven, and I were cordial with him.

When the weekend came, the real Jim showed up. Jim was an alcoholic, and when he drinks, he becomes a whole nother person. He was very verbally and physically abusive toward my mother. Every weekend, my siblings and I had to witness this type of behavior. However, Saul and other family members put a beating on Jim on a regular basis.

My siblings and I endured so much, and I thank God that we were able to overcome that catastrophe together. When he was not drunk, he was quiet and stayed in the bedroom. We even witnessed Jim stabbing another man.

One day, when Jim came home from work and my mother wasn't home, he was yelling all through the house, calling her name. He messed up the house so badly by throwing all our furniture and hollering out our names. My big brother Saul wasn't home when all of this was going on. Nelly, Daven, and I climbed out the back window and hid on the roof just outside our bedroom until he left.

When my mother came home and found out what was going on, that was the last we saw of Jim because my mother put him out.

All I can do is thank God for always being with us! The push from our mother, although she was not home regularly, helped lead us in the right direction. Although our mother had a rough time dealing with Jim, I must say she made sure all four of us were fed, well dressed, and well taken care of. My mother also ensured that we all graduated through high school. I would not take anything away from my experiences because they showed me what to do, and not to do, when I became a mother.

We have always been a pretty tight-knit family. I was especially close to Daven growing up as children when Kitten

CANDIA J. OLIVER

started hanging out with us. She was light-skinned, medium-height with long ponytails, and very slim. Kitten lived two doors from me. I introduced Doris to Kitten, and we all became very close friends, but I noticed continuous drama issues. Kitten would say Doris was negatively talking about me, and Doris would say vice versa. Kitten came to me and said,

"Girl Doris been talking about you to Patsy and Nutty. Girl, she is a trip and supposed to be your best friend."

Kitten would never say exactly what Doris was supposed to have said. I figured Kitten told the truth, considering Doris hung around Patsy and Nutty and I noticed she was changing, presumably under their influence. Kitten and I became closer over time, but she did many sneaky things that eventually caused me to lose trust in her.

One day, my brother Daven acted like he was Kitten's cousin, Pinky, and called Kitten. Daven changed his voice and asked Kitten,

"What do you think about that girl, Candy, you hang around with?"

"Girl, she is alright—I just go down to her house when I don't have anything to do. Girl, her sister and brother always cook, and I go down there to eat," Daven said.

"OH, you go down there to freeload off of them?"

"Girl, yeah."

Daven hung up the phone and said,

"We need to go right down to her house now so you can beat her up."

We did, and I beat Kitten up really badly. There I was, doing anything Daven felt I should do. After that, I stopped hanging out with Kitten. I had many back-and-forth female friendships, which usually happens during this stage of adolescence. Overall, we all still remained friends, but Doris was the one I preferred to be around since she was my best friend.

Daven was over-protective of me. I tell you, he drove me crazy at times! I used to try to duck him out sometimes so he could not follow me. However, his over-protectiveness paid off. If I had escaped with half of the things I tried to do, I probably would not be where I am today. I probably would have had five children, abused drugs, and Lord knows what else I would have done!

When my kids were younger, they reminded me of Daven and me. It really amazes me to see how they act just like we did. Chevy is a Taurus like Daven, and Ray is a Libra like me. I think this is so interesting. I love my other brothers and sisters, but Daven and I have always been there for each other —I guess it's because we are so close in age, not counting the other four children my father has.

2

FIRST LOVE AND GROWING PAINS

When Doris and I started middle school, we no longer shared the same classes until the 8th grade. Ms. Sharpen was our homeroom and our science teacher. That was one of the best school years I had. I really was a class clown, and we had many fun people in our class, such as Janet, Rainee, and Esther. We had so much fun that we frequently found ourselves in trouble—especially me.

One day, Doris, Janet, Rainee, Esther, and I decided that we were going to hang out in the hall before going to class. Ms. Sharpen locked us out of the class for the entire class period.

I always had the gift of making people laugh, and that also applied to my classmates. It happens naturally without much effort.

Daven told me one night,

"You should wear a pair of mommy's old shoes to school. I will pick out the shoes; I know you would have your class laughing."

Of course, I did it. The next day, I walked into class with a pair of my mother's old black platform shoes made in the early 70s and some tight jeans. We all entered our homeroom class so we could be dismissed, and the whole class was quiet. I slammed my foot on the desk, and everyone turned around, saw those shoes, and started laughing. Even Ms. Sharpen laughed; however, I noticed that she allowed everyone to leave the room except for me. It was at that moment that I realized I made a huge mistake! Consequently, she reported me to my mother, Joyce, on the phone, and let's just say that didn't end well! When I came home from school, my mother called my name

"Candia Joyette Oliver,"

walking downstairs, and I knew that if she called my full government name—I knew then I was in major trouble!

My mother said,

"Your teacher called me and said you were showing off in school, get up these steps!"

My mom beat me so badly with a belt. I was unable to sit properly in the chair the next day in school. But of course, I still did not learn my lesson! I think I used to act up in school for attention from my teachers.

On December 16, 1980, I met Levi during my 8th-grade year. Levi was short, brown-skinned, handsome, bow-legged, had a nice haircut, and was dressed so neatly. I love a short man. Doris, Janet, Rainee, Ester, and I were returning from lunch and walking down the hall headed to Mr. Miara's typing class.

"Look at him, he is so bow-legged and fine," I said to my girlfriends.

"Girl, I want him," Ester said.

"Uh, he's mine," I said, walking near him and purposely bumping into Levi.

"Girl, you need to watch where you are going," he said.

"Excusee meee," I asked defensively.

"What is your name?"

"Levi."

"My name is Candy."

We then proceeded to our typing class, and Levi went to his class. About half an hour later, this boy Oscar came into my class and threw a piece of paper in our class, and declared that it was for me. I picked it up and glanced over it, and it had Levi's name and phone number. I told my friends, and they asked if I was going to call him. I said, "Probably so."

The bell rang for all students to go home. As I left the building, I ran into Levi again near the stairs.

"Where are you going?" I asked.

"I'm going to work," he answered, as I was genuinely shocked and impressed because it was rare to meet guys in school with a job. Normally, we all had our summer jobs, but he worked during the school year, which was amazing to me.

"Where do you work?"

"Cross Street Market at Taylor's Meats."

I was not familiar with that area, but I wondered what time he left work so I would know when to call him.

"Just call around 9:00 pm," he declared.

"Okay."

At approximately 9:00 p.m. that same night, I dialed the phone number and received a quick response.

"Hello," a baritone voice answered.

"Hi, may I speak to Levi?" I asked.

"Boo Boo—come get the phone," the deep voice yelled.

"Hello," Levi answered seconds later.

"Who was that?"

"Oh, just my brother!" Little did he know that I was aware it was Levi who initially answered the phone; he just changed his voice to make it sound deeper to mask that it wasn't him who answered the phone. I still have no idea why he went through all of that!

"Levi, I know that was you who answered the phone, and you tried to change your voice."

"No, that was my brother!"

"You came to the phone too fast for your brother to scream your name like that," I said, which proceeded into a nice general conversation between Levi and me, so I invited him to my house.

The next day, there was a knock on the front door as my mom and I were in the kitchen. I became nervous when I opened the door, and Levi looked so handsome. I introduced Levi to my mother, Joyce, and he sat down beside me, and he was just as nervous. Levi repeatedly rubbed his legs with his hands, rocking back and forth.

"What is wrong?"

"Nothing," he answered, as I realized it was after 9:00 p.m.

"Well, it's getting late and I have to get ready for school," I lied, because I assumed he was crazy after witnessing him rock back & forth.

He finally left my house, and I was relieved to close the door behind him.

"He will never visit here again! Something was wrong with him," I said directly to my mom standing in the kitchen.

"Levi was just nervous, but he seems like a nice guy and I think you should stick with him," she declared.

"Okay, maybe I'll let him come over one more time."

My mother felt in her heart that Levi was a pretty good guy because he was very respectful when he greeted my mother.

I called Levi and invited him back over the following night, and he wasn't as nervous as the night before. I wondered when he would try to kiss me. He finally tried, then backed up.

"Wait a minute, I have to take my watch off because it's keeping me from kissing you," he said.

I immediately thought to myself that this boy is crazy.

"How is your watch preventing you from kissing me?"

"I don't know," he said, throwing his silver watch on the coffee table beside him.

I shook my head and walked Levi to the door to leave.

"Would you like to go to the movies with me on Sunday?"

I was in shock because no guy ever asked me to go to the movies before.

"Are you joking? You are not taking me to the movies!"

"Yes, I am," he exclaimed, as if he were saying, "Damn, you've never been to the movies before?"

"Okay, what time should I be ready?"

"Once I leave the church, which is around 12:00 p.m., I will come and pick you up!"

When Sunday morning arrived, I was so excited, and I felt a drop in my stomach. I couldn't believe I was going out on a date. It was a beautiful day, and I had my hair all done up with my jean outfit on. My mother told me to make sure I had some carfare and 25 cents to call her, just in case something went wrong.

Levi came to pick me up on time. He looked handsome with a nice haircut and had on a nice outfit. We caught the bus, 28 Cherry Hill, and only had to pay 50 cents.

Our first movie together was "Stir Crazy." The movie was packed. Levi bought me popcorn, a hotdog, and a soda, and bought himself some Raisinets. We sat down in the theater, and although Levi was scared to hug me at first, he finally did.

After the movie was over, we went to Peccadillo to get pizza on Howard Street. Levi was a pizza lover.

As my relationship with Levi developed and we started spending more time together, my friendship with Doris made a drastic change. I do not know if it was because we were not hanging out as much—I really did not know. Doris did not really express her feelings. One day in school, Doris showed a different side of herself in front of other girlfriends in our English class. She became sassy with me and got smart, which I think the other girls instigated her to do.

"Doris, you better leave me alone because you are starting to get on my nerves," I yelled, yet she continued to antagonize me.

When the school bell rang for us to change classes, I hit Doris and we began passing hits. Ms. Jones and the vice principal, Mr. Bright, broke the fight up. The fight resulted in me receiving a full-day suspension because I hit Doris first, and she was only sent home for the remainder of the day.

When I arrived home, I cried to my mother because I was sad that Doris and I fought each other. My mom advised me to walk to Doris's house to make amends. I followed her advice and noticed Mrs. Wilkens sitting on the porch with Doris, and she was so upset with us. I was so nervous and upset with myself when I approached their house.

Mrs. Wilkens said to me and Doris,

"You both were wrong, you two should be ashamed of yourselves!"

Doris and I still hung around each other, but you could tell there was a huge difference in our friendship. I felt an awkwardness in my heart, body, and soul. I felt it during our hug because we both knew we were wrong.

As time progressed, Levi and I grew closer, and he would come to my house every day straight from work. On January

9, 1981, we decided to become boyfriend and girlfriend. February 7, 1981, marked our first time being sexually active before we went to the Sugar Hill Gang Show at the Civic Center. We started kissing, and then we went to the next step, having sex on my mother's living room couch. We did make it to the show after.

Every Sunday, we would wait for Levi's mother to leave to go to church; we would eat breakfast and have sex, then we would go to the movies. This was our Sunday routine for years.

Levi finally introduced me to his mother. Ms. Dorothy was pretty, with brown skin, a beautiful smile, short, heavy set, and a sweet woman. I also met his sisters, Sherri, Roe, and his brother, Donnie. I became very close with Ms. Dorothy; she loved for me to call her on the telephone to make her laugh.

Levi began buying me clothes and giving me money. I would go shopping for us and purchase matching outfits for a guy and a girl. We were only 14, but from that point on, my mother never had to buy clothes for me again!

Levi and I both were at a point in our relationship where we felt as though we were going to be together forever. We went to the same high school: Carver Vocational-Technical High School. Carver is both a career technology center and a college preparatory high school, preparing students for college and careers. Levi's trade was bricklaying, and my trade was data processing. The bricklayer's trade consists of laying bricks, concrete blocks, stone, and other similar materials to construct or repair. The data processing trade consists of collecting data and changing the format in which the data has been presented to you.

My first year at Carver went well, but I still talked a lot in school. "Candia, your mouth is going to get you in a world of trouble," my teacher, Ms. Swin, would say.

She was right. I love to talk, but my mouth didn't always get me in trouble. I still love to talk, but not as much now—that's why I enjoy going out to stores, where I can spontaneously strike up conversations with people. However, I did cut back on my talking, depending on whom I was speaking with. I became bored with my relationship with Levi, so I secretly saw other guys. I felt that Levi always knew or sensed it, but wouldn't mention it to me.

My mother had just told me that morning I could not go over to my Aunt Peg's house. Here I go again, getting myself into something. I snuck over to my aunt's house to see my ex-boyfriend Danny, who passed away years ago. Danny was medium height, chocolate, and handsome.

"Candy, can you go downtown with me after school to pay my sister's phone bill?" my friend Janet asked.

"Ok," I said.

Once we arrived downtown, I bought myself a pair of jelly shoes. They were made out of plastic and came in a variety of colors.

"Janet, do you want to go over to Danny's house with me?" I asked.

"Sure," she said.

After Janet and I were done downtown, we caught the 15 Overlea Bus to get to Danny's house, which was down the street from my Aunt Peg's house. I wanted to introduce Janet to Danny and Trey. Trey is my Aunt Peg's daughter—and although Aunt Peg was really our cousin through marriage, my mother told my siblings and me to call her Aunt Peg—Trey is the one who introduced me to Danny. Even though we were not together anymore, I went over there this one time to see him.

"Danny, call my cousin Trey and tell her to come down to your house, and don't tell my Aunt Peg that I'm over here."

I had Danny call my cousin because I hadn't seen her in a while and I wanted to catch up with her while I was down there. I didn't want my Aunt Peg to know, because I had snuck over there despite my mother's instructions not to go.

Unfortunately, Aunt Peg already saw me down the street from where she lived. I thought I was being slick, showing off for my friend Janet. But my plans didn't go the way I thought they would. Trey never made it to Danny's house because my Aunt Peg overheard us talking and told me to go home.

When I arrived home after 6 p.m., there was a sudden knock on the door. It was the meat man. In the '80s, different meat companies would come out to your home to sell various types of meats.

"We don't want no meat!" I shouted as I marched through the hallway.

I guess my mother heard me yelling at the meat man because, next thing I knew, I heard her voice yelling—

"Candia Joyette Oliver!"

Uh-oh, I thought... here we go—I was in major trouble! My mother turned to Janet and said,

"And Janet, little girl, you can go home."

Janet didn't waste any time. She knew my mother was no joke! The tone of my mother's voice had us both petrified—you could tell by how fast Janet spun around and hurried out the door. Before I could fully grasp what was happening, my mother grabbed one of my jelly shoes out of the box and started beating me with the shoe all the way upstairs.

"Take off all of your clothes, Joyette," she yelled, as my brother Daven stood on the side of her, instigating.

"Ma, she is getting too grown! You need to beat her!"

"Daven, go to your room before I beat your butt!"

Truth is, Daven rarely got beatings because he was one of them "goody two-shoes." Daven always did what he was supposed to do, so he didn't get in any trouble. My mother tore my butt up that day, and that was my last beating with a belt. Make no mistake—I needed that a** whooping because it stopped me in my tracks and got my attention. All the talking my mother was doing just wasn't working. At the rate I was going, anything could have happened to me. I don't know where I'd be today if she hadn't knocked some sense into my head that night! My mother did not play, and I still respect her today for doing what was needed in order to keep me in line! I've learned that when raising kids, you must sometimes take drastic measures to teach them life lessons and keep them on the straight and narrow. I was punished that whole week, and I had to call Levi and tell him I couldn't have any calls for that week.

"But why?" Levi asked.

I knew I couldn't tell him the real reason was because I snuck out to see Danny. I believe that Levi grew suspicious and tired of me sneaking around, and he had been acting funny toward me by not keeping up with me the way he usually does. One morning, we entered Carver's building, and I saw this girl with these passion marks all over her neck. She was light-skinned, cute with short hair, and nicely shaped.

"Look, Levi, you know she doesn't make any sense with all these marks all over her neck," I said.

"Hmmm…" he said. I thought that was weird of him, as we separately went to our classes.

Then I realized I'd forgotten to give Levi my coat to put in his locker, so I went upstairs to his classroom—and what did I see? Levi in the hallway examining the girl with the passion marks on her neck. I could not believe my eyes, and my heart dropped to the floor. They both noticed me, and she ran to her class. Levi's eyes popped out of his head, and he was so scared because he knew how angry I was and that I was going to curse him out.

"Did you put marks on her neck?"

"Of course, not," he declared.

"You must be jealous—that's why you didn't say much about her neck when I pointed it out to you earlier."

I was confident Levi didn't put those marks on her because he was not that type of guy, but I thought to ask (in case). I never did have a problem with Levi stepping out of our relationship—it was always me. I asked Levi her name, and he said,

"Krissy."

I told Levi I wanted him to stay away from her, and he said,

"Ok."

Well, the very next day I saw him talking to her again. I warned Levi not to talk to her, and he told me he couldn't. I could not believe he told me he couldn't. I cannot stand that word today; I really thought he was crazy.

On the night of November 4, 1983, Levi went home straight from work and, usually, he would come to my house after work. I decided to call Levi while I was washing dishes.

"When are you coming over?"

"I will be there soon!"

I got tired of waiting, and I said to myself that I was going to break up with him. I walked down to Levi's house, and when I got there, he was listening to El DeBarge's "Love Me in a Special Way" and counting his money.

"I think we need to break up."

"Yes, I think we do," Levi said, and it left me in total shock and disbelief.

Not Levi telling me this! I was accustomed to being the one to break up with someone and then get back together. I initially felt that I could do without Levi, and it wouldn't matter. Well, that incident proved me wrong! I was so hurt and devastated. I don't know if it was because of my pride, or if I realized I really did love Levi. I lost weight and started doing unusual things by staying in the house and going out only when it was necessary. I wasn't my fun, outgoing self anymore. My mother and brother Daven had a really hard time seeing me like that.

The next day after we broke up, when I went to school, this guy named Fester, who lived up the street from me, gave me a boy named Eric's phone number. Eric was tall, brown-skinned, sexy, dressed very nicely, and appeared to have a nice personality. At the time, I didn't want to deal with anyone, but a couple of days later I decided to call Eric. I invited him over and introduced him to my family. My mother felt that Eric was a pretty nice guy, but he wanted a relationship and I did not. However, he insisted on trying to make it work. I would see Levi leaving school to go to work, and I would follow him to start a fight with him. I would harass Levi on a regular basis for attention, but I knew I could not continue in that manner. As a result, I had to learn to control my feelings for Levi since it seemed as though Levi didn't have an interest in me anymore.

Once I realized it was time for me to gain control of my life again, I decided to invite Eric over to my house again when I came home from school. When Eric came over, I told him I decided that I'm definitely not going back to Levi. I would like to try out a relationship with him. That's what I thought. Eric was so happy to hear those words, which I really felt at the time. However, a few minutes later the phone rang; it was Levi, so I went into the kitchen.

"Can I come over once I get off from work?"

I didn't know what to say, but I looked into the living room, and Eric got up and left. After that, I did not see or hear from Eric again.

Levi came over once he got off from work. He was very nervous and scared. Levi knew my mother and my brother Daven were upset with him because he hurt their baby (me). Not knowing all the mischief their baby had done. Daven and my mother were unaware that I dated other guys while I was with Levi. My mother's rule was that whoever we considered being our boyfriend or girlfriend, no other person was allowed to call or come over to our house except the person we were dating. Which meant, I had to sneak and do my "thing." Now, don't get me wrong—my mother could look right through all 4 of her children and know when we were up to no good. However, everyone was happy to see Levi, and so was I. Levi and I started dating again, and we were getting along and things seemed fine, but here I go again.

One evening, I was walking to the store—it was getting dark outside—when I heard a guy calling my name.

"I said, 'Who is that?'"

It sounded like a man's voice.

"I said, 'Who's that yelling my name out like that?'"

He replied, "Vic."

"Can I speak to you for a second?"

As I moved in closer, I said, "Hi, Vic."

He continued, "Give me your phone so I can take you out to dinner."

"I have a boyfriend."

"I have a girlfriend too. We can just hang out sometimes."

"Ok, and I gave him my phone number."

Vic was 22 years old, tall, brown-skinned, with broad shoulders, and sexy. He was 5 years older than me and had so much swag. I never dated an older guy, which really scared me, because my rule was I would not date anyone more than 2 years older than me. I was afraid to date older guys because I thought I wouldn't be able to handle them sexually. I expected him to be advanced and know way more about life, but to my surprise, there was no difference dealing with him than with any other guy I talked to. However, Vic happened to be a great experience for me, but I knew this couldn't last too long because of Levi, and Vic had a girlfriend too.

One night, we went out to dinner in Columbia, Maryland. I told Vic that it would be best to end our relationship because it was too risky.

"This isn't going anywhere," I told him. "You're not leaving your girlfriend, and I love Levi."

Vic nodded and said, "You're right."

And just like that, I never saw Vic again.

3

ADULTHOOD, MARRIAGE & MOTHERHOOD

This is a huge decision-making time in life once you graduate as far as what's next in your future. In June 1985, I knew it was time for me to make some changes with myself because I was stepping into the next phase of my life. I graduated from Carver Vocational-Technical High School and continued my education at Strayer Business College in October 1985. Levi was having problems finding a job as a bricklayer.

My mother said,

"Levi, you can join the military."

He said,

"I never thought about that."

I said,

"Levi, I can help you find out what you need to do."

Levi said,

"Ok."

On February 7, 1986, Levi joined the United States Marine Corps. I completed Strayer Business College with an Associate Degree in Human Services Mental Health and was on the Dean's List. Without any marriage proposal, Levi and I decided to get married once he finished boot camp. Levi and I went to the courthouse alone, and we were married on May 9, 1986. We had lunch afterward at Rusty Scupper Restaurant. Levi left home two weeks later to go to military school in Albany, Georgia. Once Levi reached Albany, Georgia, he began looking for housing, which took a month. I was so eager to move to Georgia because my mother drove me crazy with her fussing all the time. I joined Levi in Albany, Georgia, from June 1986 until September 1986.

However, when it was time for me to leave Baltimore, my mother, brother Daven, and I cried horribly—you would have thought someone had died. My big brother Saul drove me to the airport, and it was my first time ever leaving home and flying on an airplane. This had to be one of the worst flying experiences a person could ever endure. First, I had a layover in Atlanta, Georgia, and then it was time to board the next plane. We had to exit the plane on the runway because of a technicality.

When I heard that the plane was having technical problems, the first thing that came to my mind was that I needed to get off this plane right away! I didn't care if I needed to jump off that plane. I was silently panicking as everyone was trying to get their luggage and holding up the line to get off the plane. I pushed my way through the crowd, saying, "Excuse me, excuse me," until I finally made it off. I think I was in fight-or-flight mode.

Southwest Airlines gave us the option to stay in Atlanta, Georgia, or board another flight that was arriving in Albany, Georgia. Imagine this being my first flight ever, yeah right! To make things even worse, I had no way to inform Levi that my flight was arriving at a later time. I spoke to a Southwest Airlines supervisor to call Albany's airport and inform my husband about this unfortunate incident. Levi did receive the message, but when I arrived in Albany, I was unable to retrieve my luggage due to the changing of flights. I did not receive my luggage until a week later, so you know that is a huge problem for a woman. Between not having my luggage and being afraid to leave home in the first place, I was extra happy to see my Levi—but in the back of my mind, I was saying to myself, "I knew I should have stayed home. I should have just waited for Levi to finish school and moved once we moved to North Carolina." Levi took me shopping to replace the major items that I needed.

We lived in a furnished trailer home—something I had never seen before, which was fine. The trailer looked like the ones that you can hook on the back of a truck, but our trailer was a parked home made of steel. The inside of the trailer was made of wood, fully furnished with the living room and kitchen in the same area. The bedroom was large down the hall from the living room and kitchen.

I enjoyed married life until I began missing my mother, brothers, sister, nieces, and best friends, Doris and Moca. Now, as I said, "I have never been away from home." My homesickness affected me drastically, which caused me to drive Levi crazy. I used to lay across the bed, bang my feet on our trailer house, cry, and keep saying I want to go home. Levi knew I really wanted to go home, so he allowed me to act out. I really tried to stick beside my husband, but I couldn't take it any longer—I had to go home! Albany was supposedly considered my home, but not in my book.

Levi said, "I had enough! You are my wife, you are supposed to be here with me, but you can go home. I know it must be hard for you." Frustrated with my antics, he packed up my bags and sat them by the door. I started crying because I felt like he was putting me out, but what could I expect if I was going to keep driving him crazy about going home? I ran out the door and went to a pay phone because it was the only phone I had access to call my mother. Levi walked behind me all the way to the pay phone. I was shocked that he had my bags packed at the door, because Levi usually doesn't say or do anything when I'm acting out about something. But this time he caught me off guard—it felt like I lost my power.

I said, "Ma, Levi is putting me out." Levi came behind me.

My mother said, "What!!! Put him on the phone."

Levi said, "Ms. Joyce, I'm not putting Candy out. She said she wanted to come home."

Mommy said, "I knew darn well you weren't putting Joy out."

I promised Levi that I would be a real wife when we moved to North Carolina, but we had to come home every holiday and my nieces had to come every summer. Levi agreed, and about 2 weeks later he let me go home.

I caught the bus home—it felt safer to take the bus, and I did not care how long the ride was. It was a 24-hour ride, and for some reason, my jeans felt much tighter, making me uncomfortable.

Once I reached home at 2 a.m., my mother was asleep, and Daven was nowhere to be found. I was so upset with Daven because I missed him so much. Since my mother was asleep and my brother was gone, I decided to go over to Doris's house. I was so excited about being home that I even caught a cab. Doris lived around the corner from my house. I went around the back of her house and threw a rock at her window—and she woke up and opened the door.

Doris and I sat and talked all morning long about my experience in Albany, Georgia. Later that morning, I called Moca and my sister-in-law Lisa to catch up with them. Moca was my other best friend. We met while attending Strayer Business College.

Moca is light-skinned, pretty, with thick black hair, and of medium height. I enjoyed spending time with Moca because she loved to laugh. Moca thought I was so funny, which was just in my nature. People still laugh at the way and how I say things. Moca was a godly woman, and she taught me the meaning of discernment.

One day, I was telling her, "I feel like I am psychic, because I can meet a person one time and I can feel them," and that is when she told me that what I'm describing is called discernment.

Moca said, "Would you like to drive to Kings Dominion with me and my boyfriend?"

I said, "Sure, if my niece Keio can come along."

Moca said, "Yes."

I had the nerve to go to Kings Dominion—which is a three-hour drive—after just getting off a 24-hour bus ride, but I didn't care; I was just excited to be home. I must say, I enjoyed being with my niece, whom I had not seen in what seemed like forever.

My mother finally saw me the next day. My mother said, "You sure look different—are you pregnant?"

Levi came home for 2 weeks after finishing school in Albany. I told him I made a doctor's appointment to see if I was pregnant because I did notice that I had put on a few pounds. It never crossed my mind that I was pregnant. However, Levi and I went to my doctor's appointment, and the verdict was in: I was pregnant. It's crazy how intuitive mothers are with their children, being able to feel and know their child inside out. We were so happy to discover we were pregnant with our first child, but I tell you, I was in shock. I began to experience challenges with my body— eczema broke out all over. Levi had to report to Marine Corps Base Camp Lejeune, North Carolina, where he was stationed while I stayed home until Levi found housing for us.

Well, as I told Levi once we moved to North Carolina, I would not ask to return to Baltimore for a while, anyway. This time, I had a non-stop flight, which was excellent because I was pregnant. I sure did not need a repeat episode from when I flew to Albany. I moved to North Carolina in January 1987, and it was so beautiful and peaceful that I could hardly believe it. We had a beautiful two-bedroom home—very spacious and comfortable. You needed a car to live there because the stores were a long distance from our house. Levi taught me how to drive while living in NC because I did not want to depend on him to do all the driving. It was nice to get away from the busyness in Baltimore. I was ready for this type of living. Now, don't get me wrong—I love my Cherry Hill because that is where I got my foundation. It was time to move on into a different phase in my life with becoming a mother and a wife. I said to myself, "Oh, I think I'm going to like this," and I did.

I felt very comfortable, and Levi introduced me to this couple, Sandy and Rick, and we hit it off right away. Sandy is light, medium-height, and pretty, and Rick is tall, brown-skinned, and nice-looking. This couple had a lot in common with us, especially in being married and settled.

Levi and I got married on May 9, and Sandy and Rick got married on May 12. I tell you—Sandy and I had so much fun together! We used to go to the parties on the base and jam off our song "Rock The Bells" by LL Cool J. Levi and Sandy were the calmer ones, but when it was just Sandy and me, I would bring the fun side of her out. Rick and I also had a ball together, acting crazy and cracking jokes about one another. Our spouses knew Rick and I were going to turn it up when we got together.

However, Sandy and Rick are no longer married, but I still keep in touch with Sandy today. They broke up once Levi and Rick completed the military. We all returned back home. Levi and I went back to Baltimore, and they returned back to New Orleans. We all said that we would remain in touch, and Sandy is like a sister to me to this day.

I visit with her and the family, and her new husband, in New Orleans every spring. I also visit Rick while I'm there, and I love them all so dearly. Rick and Sandy have a better relationship now because they have two sons together. So, whenever I come to town, Sandy lets Rick know, and he comes over to her house to see me.

In April, Levi and I drove home to Baltimore for the Easter holiday. As I told Levi, I have to return home for every holiday. Our baby's due date was in May, and my doctor advised against me traveling home so close to my due date."I said to myself,

'Yeah, right. I'm going home!'

Levi said, 'Candy, you hear what the doctor said?'

I told Levi, 'We are going to Baltimore. I will be just fine.'"

We drove down, listening to music the entire drive, and my focus was on getting home to see my family. We had to make many stops for me to use the bathroom, and Levi just did what he needed to do for me and the baby. We made it to Baltimore safely with my enormous tummy, and our family was happy to see us—and we were happy to see them. Levi and I enjoyed our Easter vacation, and four days later, we were on the road headed back to North Carolina.

The very next morning, Levi got ready for work while I laid in bed. Suddenly, I felt a warm liquid stream down my legs. I said to Levi,

"It feels like I'm laying here peeing on myself."

Levi, in a calm and confident tone, said,

"Your water is breaking!"

I said to him,

"Like you really know what's going on!"

When I got up, water was pouring down my legs. I said to Levi,

"Come on, we have to go now!!"

I was in labor for 10 long hours. I told myself, "When this baby arrives, he or she better not give me an ounce of trouble." We had a boy—Chevy was finally born on April 21, 1987, at Onslow Memorial Hospital in Jacksonville, North Carolina. I asked the nurse, "Is that my baby crying in the nursery?" She replied, "Yes." I said, "I am ready to see Chevy," and she brought him to me. Then I said, "Hold up, this is not my baby; this baby looks Chinese, and his father and I are black."

My mother told me to watch out for this because baby switching was occurring a lot in the '80s. If I hadn't been hard-headed, my mother would have been here with me, but Chevy came early because I took that drive up to Baltimore. The nurse said, "He is your baby—look at the wristband; it matches." I said, "Ok."

Levi just let me go for it because he already knows how I am. Chevy has these slanted eyes, and real, real light, and Levi and I are brown skin… I just didn't understand. Well, I truly forgot I have slanted eyes; eventually, he would become a little darker. Chevy had my mother's complexion, but I wasn't thinking that a child could inherit some of their grandparent's genes. The only thing stuck in my head what my mother made me aware of. However, Chevy was definitely our child! Chevy looks just like both of us. I told my mother what happened and sent her some pictures. My mother said,

"Joy, he looks just like you, you think you're ugly or something?"

My mother calls me by my middle name.

Levi and I returned home to Baltimore in 1989 because Levi had to report overseas to finish his term in the Marine Corps in Okinawa, Japan. Chevy and I did not travel along with Levi. There was no way I was going to move to another country, and I could barely adapt to living in another state. Before Levi left to finish his term in Japan, we discovered that I was pregnant (yet again).

It was very easy to raise Chevy, so we both agreed we wanted another child. We both wanted a boy and a girl. I was so happy, but I noticed that each time Levi was stationed elsewhere—he ensured I was pregnant while he was away. Like I said before when I was pregnant with Chevy, I experienced numerous changes within my body.

Well, here we go again—when I was 8 months pregnant with the new baby, I suffered from sinus issues. My doctor was unable to prescribe me any medications due to the pregnancy (and I eventually had three sinus operations after my second pregnancy).

I'll be the first to admit that I was a nuisance. My older sister Nelly and Daven were tired of me thinking I was in labor. It came to the point where they would look through the peephole of their door to see if it was me—and they would not answer the door if it was. Now that was a hot mess; I wasn't that much of a nuisance. One time, I found out Nelly was going to see a movie, so I got Chevy and dressed quickly, then rushed downtown to go with her. When we left the theater, my car was gone—it had been towed away because I parked in a tow zone while rushing to be with Nelly. Mind you, all this was happening while I was pregnant and had Chevy with me. Imagine that.

Nelly was so upset with me and said,

"You should have stayed home in the first place, and I wouldn't be having to go through all of this."

It was like Daven and Nelly had forgotten that Levi was in Japan—and that I needed them. Well, I didn't have to worry about that anymore because I told my mother how Daven and Nelly treated me. My mother said,

"Joy, don't pay them any mind, you know how they can be—you can just call your mother. Lance and I will look after you."

Lance was my mom's boyfriend at that time, they'd been together since 1985. Lance is light-skinned, medium-built, and handsome. My mother and Lance finally got married on November 14, 2023, after being together for 39 years. My mother said,

"Even though you might as well say we are married because Lance gave me a ring years ago... I will be 80 years old in April, and I want to put his name on the lease just in case anything happens to me. I want to make sure Lance always has a place to live."

One day, as I was headed out the front door to go to the shopping center, she told us that he was coming to the house. When I started walking, I noticed this man coming toward me. He asked,

"Do you know a lady named Joycee?"

I already knew my mother was waiting for him, so I said,

"Yes, that's my mother."

Curious to see how they were together, I walked back with Lance to our house.

My mom realized what Daven and Nelly were talking about quickly because I thought I was in labor every week. One day, I thought I was in labor, and mommy and Lance took me to John Hopkins University Hospital. Eventually, I found out that I experienced premature labor pains, which had occurred a previous time. It came to the point where my mom was flustered from the back and forth to the hospital. My mother said,

"Joy, this is what we are going to do—I'm going to stay at your house with you and Chevy until you have this baby!"

The next day, we called Lance because it felt like the baby was coming through the labor pains this time. All the way to John Hopkins, I had to pull up on the grab handle in the car, and my mother was talking me through the labor pains. We made it to the hospital just in time.

Once the doctors laid me on the bed, my baby girl came right out. My Doctor Marly did not have the opportunity to deliver my baby because she came so fast.

Ray was born in October, light skin and beautiful, and looks just like her father. Levi did not get the opportunity to meet his baby girl until she was 4 months old, but I kept him updated through my entire pregnancy with numerous pictures of Chevy and me.

I tell you my mother is the greatest—she stuck with me throughout my pregnancy. My mommy always comes through for her children, and she doesn't play when it comes to us. Now I have the two most beautiful kids: a son and a daughter, and they are everything to me! That is the truth; anyone who knows me can tell you that!!! If you don't know, you better ask somebody because I do not play when it comes to my children—Levi will tell you that!

4

SELF-DISCOVERY AND THE
TURNING POINT

July 27th, 1993 marked a new era in my life at the age of 27, and I thought my growing pains would never end. I could not comprehend what I was experiencing. The summer of 1993 was one of the most difficult and traumatic summers when I came to the realization that I was attracted to women. This realization had a huge effect on my life, including my marriage with Levi and raising our two children. I thought my life was ruined forever and continuously prayed for understanding from God.

It all began when I met my high school friend Terri, who lived up the street from me. She was a tall, brown-skinned woman with long, pretty, black hair and pretty teeth. I would enjoy her presence when she returned home from work because she was always well dressed. However, if I had known I was attracted to women, Terri would not have been my first choice—but I found myself caught in a rapture. In other words, I was never interested in dating anyone who was taller than I was in case I needed to whoop his or her ass—I'm just saying!

I attempted to distance myself from my hidden feelings

toward Terri. There was a point when I believed that I felt this way because I had two female best friends, was hurt by one of them, and was on the verge of being hurt by the other. The last thing I wanted was another friend who could hurt me, so I thought if I kept my distance from my feelings everything would be okay. My best friend Moca didn't speak to me for 10 years after I told her I was attracted to Terri. I thought my other best friend didn't care about me anymore. Now that I am older, I am able to understand that friendships change. It doesn't necessarily mean that your friend doesn't care about you anymore—and that's the way I was looking at it back then.

One day, I asked Terri to go with me to PetSmart so I could get Chevy a rabbit for his birthday.

"Rabbit? I will get it for him," Terri said.

I brought the rabbit home, and Chevy was so happy. I told him, "Let's name her Lucky."

Lucky and my dog, CJ didn't get along the first couple of days after I brought CJ home. CJ started going over to Lucky's cage, putting his nose inside, and Lucky would come up and put her nose in too. They began to bond, and eventually I was able to let Lucky out of the cage so they could run around the house together.

Lucky lived until she was 10 years old, and we buried her in the back of our house in Middle River, Maryland. When CJ went outside to use the bathroom, he would always go over and sniff where Lucky was buried.

While riding to PetSmart with Terri, I became argumentative with her for no apparent reason, falling into a pattern of starting arguments with her. I also grew accustomed to being ignored by her since she was non-confrontational. One day, we were going shopping, and I felt that Terri was taking the long route to get there. So I began arguing with her, but of course, she didn't pay me any mind—she just kept driving. I think it was a defense mechanism I used to prevent myself from expressing my true feelings.

Terri eventually became upset and confronted me for the way I treated her. It initially shocked me, but it was rather refreshing to witness Terri defend herself for the first time. I understood her viewpoint and apologized to her. I realized I couldn't continue treating her that way because of the experiences I'd had with other friends. I didn't like how I felt when my best friend stopped talking to me and mistreated me. So, what right did I have to mistreat Terri? Reflecting on it, I began to consider where my behavior toward her might have stemmed from.

During that summer, many of my family members and close friends were all experiencing various trials and tribulations, and naturally, being an empath, I found myself taking on other people's problems as my own. My brother Saul and his wife Lisa were going through a separation, and Terri discovered her husband was seeing another woman for the past two years of their marriage. I didn't like what was happening in both of their relationships, and it affected me to hear about what they were going through. It was during that time that Terri and I's friendship flourished, and I finally let my guard down.

I began feeling concerned for Terri's well-being and thought I at least owed that to her since I was not a good friend in the past. In retrospect, that is how I perceived the situation. That same summer, Terri taught me how to draw, and I was totally unaware I metaphorically became the one "she drew in."

We would sit on the porch at night, conversing, laughing, and sharing our emotions with each other. The first movie Terri and I went to see was The Bodyguard with Whitney

Houston, which was released on November 25, 1992. I had always admired Whitney Houston—she was my first love, in a way. Watching her on the big screen was unforgettable, and sharing that moment with Terri only made it more special.

Terri and I would meet for lunch at the docks near my job at Middle Branch Park in Cherry Hill. I always wondered why Terri would come and eat lunch with me so often, and it prompted me to ask, "I really enjoy the food at your job's cafeteria," she responded.

I did not quite believe her, but I accepted her answer with a grain of salt. I never knew how far her job was from mine until one day I asked Terri to take me to her job. We were just driving and driving, and I asked Terri,

"Girl, when are we going to get to your job?"

Terri said,

"We will be there soon."

When we finally made it to her job, I was in shock. Terri worked in Owings Mills, and I could not believe it. There was no way I would have come so far on a regular basis to have lunch with a girlfriend. The distance from Cherry Hill to Owings Mills, going through the city, took us about 1 hour. I said,

"Girl, you come this far to have lunch with me. Girl, I'm going to tell you right now: I'm not coming this far to have lunch with you or anyone else. This is too far."

Around the second week of July, my best friend Moca and I planned to visit her aunt, who lived in Virginia. Moca called me two nights before our trip and told me that her husband was going, so I suggested that they should go without me—I didn't want to feel like a third wheel. Moca disagreed that I would be the third wheel, and we got into a heated argument.

Eventually, I went to Ocean City, Maryland, with Terri for an overnight getaway. It was nice and relaxing. Ocean City is a resort town in the U.S. state of Maryland between the Atlantic Ocean and the Isle of Wight Bay. It features miles of beach and a wooden boardwalk lined with restaurants, shops, and hotels. The Assawoman Bay Bridge crosses Assawoman Bay in Ocean City. The bridge carries Maryland Route 90, a freeway, into northern Ocean City.

The water is beautiful, but I tell you this—that bridge scared the crap out of me. I do not care how beautiful it is; you will never catch me driving across that bridge. That bridge is too long and too high, so Terri did all the driving.

The sandy Atlantic shoreline is fun to explore, and the many water sports are a must at Ocean City—with surfing, fishing, and kayaking among the top activities. The weather was absolutely beautiful. We strolled along Ocean City's world-famous wooden boardwalk and enjoyed pier rides. Terri and I did not get on any rides, but we did go shopping. We also got crabs at Hooper's Crab House and brought them back to the hotel room.

Terri and I started getting comfortable. Terri undressed in front of me and put on a lace-top nightgown.

"Why would you wear something like that while staying overnight with a girlfriend?" I asked.

"There's nothing wrong with wearing a nightgown like this," she replied, as I thought to myself that I would never wear anything provocative in front of a female friend.

In contrast, I changed into my pajamas in the bathroom. Once finished, we drank strawberry daiquiris. I went to use the bathroom and noticed that I was wet before I used the bathroom. I wiped myself to see what was going on, and the tissue was wet. I even noticed that I felt "horny." I was totally in shock because I have not felt wet and horny in 7 years. That's a long time, right? I came out of the bathroom, and I admitted it to Terri.

Terri was not in disbelief because she knew a bit about my sex life with my husband Levi. You know how girlfriends talk, but I can tell you this: you better stop talking about your sex life with your friends. Since Terri already knew about what was going on with Levi and my sex life, I felt like she added icing to the cake by wearing a lace-top nightgown. I told her that I must be missing Levi, and I sure wished that I was home while feeling sexually aroused. Now, I was not thinking at this time that I was really feeling attracted to her, but I couldn't figure out what it was that I was feeling. We ate our crabs on my queen-sized bed, so when it was time to go to bed I asked Terri if it would be okay if I slept in her bed. I didn't want to sleep in my bed because the bed smelled like crabs. Terri said, "That would be fine." I told her that the only way I could fall asleep was by putting my leg on her, which was true. Looking back, I probably should have tried to sleep without doing that.

The next morning, we were getting prepared to go home, and we both seemed to be in a rush to leave. I experienced very uncomfortable and unsettling feelings—I just wanted to get back to Baltimore with Levi and my children. I had an inkling that she was aware of what I was feeling.

Terri mentioned that she wanted to stop at the grocery store, and I told her I would like to stop at the Flea Market to purchase some sheets. We went to the grocery store, but we didn't go to the Flea Market. I asked Terri,

"Why didn't we stop at the Flea Market?"

She said,

"You need to keep your money in your pocket."

"Don't tell me what I need to do with my money, you must be out of your mind," I retorted.

I was so angry because I was used to her doing anything I asked. I don't know where that came from—her trying to tell me what to do. I was trying to figure out what was wrong with her.

We did not say anything else to one another the rest of the way home. Finally, we made it home and removed our belongings from the car. I suggested that we save the other bottle of strawberry daiquiri for later that day.

Later that afternoon, my sister-in-law Lisa came over, and I offered her some of the strawberry daiquiri Terri and I had left over. I went to Terri's house to retrieve the remaining bottle and noticed the empty bottle of daiquiri in the sink. I was heated with Terri and asked her about the daiquiri.

"She said, 'Her and her husband drank it.'"

I said, "What girl are you tripping? I told you we were going to drink the other bottle later."

Terri said, "I can buy you another bottle."

It was like it was no big deal to her—they drank it and that was it. I was so hurt and disappointed with her. That was the second time she disappointed me in one day, and I could not understand why. I mentioned the situation to Lisa, and Lisa told me to just let it be; it's just a daiquiri mix. Of course, I did not see it that way, and I did not want to talk or hear from Terri anymore that day.

The next day, I woke up still feeling hurt and angry. I went out, and when I came home later that day, I went onto my front porch. I looked down the street—who did I see? Terri, sitting on her porch. She had the audacity to speak and say,

"Hi, girlfriend." I was so pissed off.

The funny thing is, I actually went onto the front porch because I knew that every day after work was when she went there, but I was not ready for her to say anything to me. Yes, these were my crazy thoughts. Truth be told, I really didn't know what was going on with me. I went back into the house and called Terri on the phone because I felt like she was really trying to take me for granted. I could tell Terri was starting to pick up on the strong feelings I had for her, and she began to take advantage of them.

I told Terri that I knew what she was doing and that I felt she was being unfair to me. Terri apologized and said,

"I can't believe your reaction to all of this, but I'm sorry I hurt your feelings."

I couldn't believe my own reaction either, and it made me start to worry about what was going on with me.

However, looking back as I've grown older, I noticed I had an interest in older, pretty women who dressed nicely. The only way I felt I could be friends with a female was if she was cute. I never could understand why I felt that way. I would always see an older woman named Ms. Jane, who had light brown skin with black and gray hair—and her hair always looked nice. Ms. Jane was always neat and had a nice physique. I always felt attracted to her, and I would always see her with a woman who wore men's clothing. I couldn't understand why she dated a woman instead of a man. Well, now I understand—because she is a lesbian.

I would love to see Ms. Jane on her way over to her sister's house—Ms. Claudy—who lived around the corner from my house. Ms. Jane and Ms. Claudy were friends of my mother; they would come over to our house every now and then to party with her. When I saw Ms. Jane, I would run over to her sister's porch to speak to her.

"Hi, Ms. Jane," I would greet her.

"Hi, Candy," she responded, appearing so excited.

When I was in the 2nd grade, her son was my boyfriend for a week. I think I had him as my boyfriend so I could get close to his mother. As time transpired, I had this feeling that one day Ms. Jane would be mine! I felt that if she had said anything to me about wanting to be with me, I would have. I felt that feeling within myself and cannot explain why.

That night, Levi and I had the most explosive argument of our 7 ½ years of marriage—one that shook us in a way we had never felt before. Levi appeared very irritated and short with me whenever I asked him a question. He even cursed at me, which was unusual, so I started cursing back. I was already very agitated, and the last thing I needed was Levi talking to me in any kind of way. I didn't like what was going on, because our kids could overhear us arguing. We never displayed that kind of behavior around our kids—they were only 3 and 5 at the time and never said anything about the fighting—but I knew it was something I didn't want around them, given my own experiences growing up.

I woke up the next morning with the worst headache you can imagine. I took six Tylenol throughout the day. Once I arrived at work, I thought the two Tylenol I took before I left home would have helped, but they did not. I sat at my desk, thinking, "What the hell is going on with me?" I decided to write Levi a letter because I express myself better on paper. In it, I admitted that I hadn't been showing him the attention I should, and that I had taken on Lisa and Terri's problems a lot lately—neglecting my role as his wife. I was internalizing their feelings, just as I did in all my friendships. All I knew was that I wanted to help them, which inadvertently brought me closer to wanting to be there for Terri.

All of a sudden, something just hit me. I couldn't explain the feeling, but it was like a voice saying, "You know that is not it—you are attracted to Terri." I jumped up out of my chair and kept repeating to myself, "No, no, no, no, do not do this to me, God, please don't!" I cried and cried, pacing the floor. I was relieved that my supervisor was in a meeting that morning, giving me the space to deal with my emotions.

I sat back down, holding my head, when the phone rang.

"Zamms Company, may I help you?" I answered.

Guess who it was? None other than Terri!!

I told her I did not feel like talking right now because I wasn't feeling too great. Terri asked what was wrong. I told her I could not discuss this with anyone—I just did not feel like talking. I thought, especially, not to her.

Terri said,

"You know we can talk about anything and everything."

I said,

"No way, I cannot talk to anyone about this."

Terri said,

"I know what it is."

I replied,

"No way."

She then said,

"Yes, I do. Girl, Levi is going to kill us."

I exclaimed,

"What!!!!!!"

I felt she must have known, but I did not say anything. I said to Terri,

"If you know, then tell me."

Terri said,

"No, I want you to tell me."

I said,

"I am getting ready to hang up this phone. Call me back at four o'clock when my supervisor leaves."

In the meantime, I called Lisa and told her I needed to talk—it was very important. Lisa holds a special place in my heart because she has always been there for me since I was 11 years old—I can tell her anything. Lisa came to my job, and I wrote her a letter because that was the only way I could explain what was going on with me. Lisa read the letter and said,

"It's nothing bad about you feeling attracted to Terri."

I felt a huge relief hearing that from someone I had always looked up to since I was a little girl—and still do. Terri called at four o'clock on the dot. I then thought of a way to ask her if she really knew what I was talking about. I said to Terri,

"If you know so much, who does it involve?"

Terri replied,

"You and I."

My head fell on my desk—I could not believe she knew. I figured Terri must have been feeling the same emotions, simultaneously. I asked her to meet me at our special place after she got off work so we could discuss what we were going to do about our situation.

Terri said,

"Ok."

5

BREAKING FREE AND FINDING STRENGTH

Terri and I still needed to discuss what we were going to do about our situation. Terri and I met at our special place, and I said,

"Terri, I can't do this to Levi."

Nothing happened between Terri and me as of yet, but I knew that it wouldn't be fair to myself if I didn't face that I was attracted to a female. I told Terri I was going to let Levi know what was going on with me as soon as I got home because I could not do this to my husband.

Terri said,

"Ok."

I experienced one of the most hurtful moments of my life because I truly loved my husband, but I also knew something was missing after giving birth to my children. It hurt me badly because I was about to break up a beautiful family— and it still breaks my heart today. I cried profusely, but I knew I had to be honest with myself and Levi, and I definitely wasn't going to have an affair in my marriage. I began seeing a therapist because this was a devastating situation for me—to have to depart from my husband. Even so, I kept my feelings to myself for about two months before I could finally talk to Levi about what I had been going through. Levi knew something was occurring with me, but he didn't know what. I shut down completely. I couldn't watch television—and if anyone knows Candy, I love some TV, hear?! The only thing that seemed to soothe me was music. I would always sit in the living room in the dark and listen to music. I entered into a depression, which caused me to lose weight. Levi would always ask me,

"What is wrong with you?"

but I would never answer—until one day.

Once I came home from work, I got Chevy, who was 5 years old at the time, and Ray, who was 3 years old, and we settled in for the evening. I told Levi we needed to talk, and I couldn't stop crying. Levi sat between my legs, and I told him, "You want to know what's wrong with me?" I opened up the blinds and said, "That's what's wrong with me."

He replied, "I don't see anything—but Terri at the park, walking her dog."

"Exactly—I'm attracted to that," I said.

Levi fell back and said, "Is that all?"

I asked, "What do you mean, 'is that all?'"

He said, "I thought you were dying."

I told Levi, "We can't be together anymore if I have feelings for a woman."

Levi couldn't understand why we couldn't stay together; he felt that since it was just a woman I was attracted to, I could be with both of them. I told him, "I'll tell you what: I'm just going to try and ignore my feelings."

Well, that didn't work, because about two weeks later we began arguing on a regular basis, which was very unusual for us. One day, Levi kept jumping in my face, trying to pick a fight—something that was very unusual. I got so frustrated that I opened the door and invited him outside because I had had enough.

"Come on outside so I whip your butt," I said.

He replied, "Ok."

He came at me, and I was very surprised. The kids were downstairs in the basement, playing with their toys. Levi actually fought me back, and we threw blows at each other. I knew this was it! Levi left and went to stay with my brother, and I talked to the kids the next day. The kids understood because they were tired of us fussing.

One day, I talked with Chevy and Ray and told them that we were moving to a new apartment. I told them that their dad and I don't want to fight around them again because it isn't pleasant. One major point I learned is not to stay in an unhealthy marriage, relationship, or whatever the case may be for the children. I say this because it is more damaging for a child to witness unhealthy behaviors in their parents. Children are very observant, and they are more resilient than you think they are.

I left the house to Levi, and we agreed that we would co-parent because our children had nothing to do with what was going on in our lives. I would have the children during the week, Levi would have them on the weekend, and we shared holidays. Levi is such an excellent father and had been an excellent husband. I apologized to Levi deeply, assuring him that my change in life did not have anything to do with him—and I didn't want him to ever think that it did. Trust me when I say, this change was sudden and it came out of nowhere.

Levi was grateful to receive my apology, and we did what we needed to do for our children. He was able to accept my apology; he knew I was an excellent wife and mother, and that I wouldn't dare try to do anything to hurt him. I loved my husband and still do today, but in a different manner. Levi has re-married twice, and I have a good relationship with them as well. I am really happy that Levi found love again.

Later in life, I noticed that Levi had made significant progress in expressing himself. His responses to questions were no longer just "yes" or "no." He seemed more confident, relying on his strength and willpower to communicate more openly. It's about what Levi wants for himself today. I am so happy to see where Levi is today, and I am thankful he is starting to live his best life. I feel like Levi deserves all the greatness that comes his way.

I came out to my family and friends. My family was really saddened about our separation and eventually our divorce. My mother told me that she wasn't shocked when I told her I was attracted to women. My mother said,

"Joy, you always was a little tomboy, and you never really wanted to wear dresses. I could just see it in you when you were a little girl."

I did like wearing dresses when Levi and I were together. My mother always taught us to be true to ourselves no matter what, and she will always love us just the way we are.

My father was upset because he said,

"You were born a girl, not a boy."

We had plenty of heated conversations about this until one day my father came over to my house and he met Petra— and he eventually let that statement go. My father liked her. Truth be told, I didn't care one way or the other because of all that I went through when I realized I was attracted to women. However, I did not face any resistance from most of my family and friends; they accepted me for who I was.

I did lose my friendship with Moca—she did not speak to me for 10 years. To this day, I still do not know why Moca stopped speaking to me. One thing I do know is that when a person reacts in that type of manner, they need to take a step back and reevaluate themselves. Eventually, Moca started speaking to me again. However, my thought process was that whoever had a problem with my lifestyle could keep it moving because no one paid my bills or took care of my children or me. All that I had to go through—mentally, emotionally, and physically—"yeah, right," they can keep it moving. My family and friends knew much was not going to change about me, just that I was with a female. Well, that is what I thought.

I would like to make something perfectly clear: I did not wake up one morning and say, "Guess what, I want to be gay." Believe me, this was the last thing I wanted to face while being married and raising two children. Many people don't understand the internal struggle I faced, not to mention the challenges Levi had to endure. I can honestly say that being gay has always been a part of who I am—it's simply how I was born.

When I was a little girl, I had a few playful, frisky experiences with other girls, but I saw it as something all children do. Looking back, I guess I had always been infatuated with pretty women. In my opinion, I feel you have the people who were born gay, the bi-sexual people, the curious gay people, and the situational gay people. What I mean about situational gay people is that they chose to be with the same sex due to some type of situation—such as they were molested or their husband or wife went out of their marriage, etc. Well, none of these examples applies to me; being gay was within me the entire time—it just happens to come out late and at the wrong time. This is how I feel. My therapist explained that the idea that all little girls engage in sexual activity with other girls is a misconception. Instead, she emphasized that being sexually involved with girls after the age of 12 is often a time when one's sexual orientation begins to develop.

I told my therapist, Helen, "I wish I had known about myself back then, because I would not have gotten married—and I wouldn't have hurt Levi." I thought about it and said, "Hold up, I wouldn't have had my children if I'd come out early." What I truly feel is that my change of life was supposed to happen in the order that it did.

Once Levi and I separated, Terri and I eventually began our relationship, and it started well. We would travel to different states and enjoy each other's company. Terri and I took Chevy and Ray to Disney World, and we had a wonderful time together. Terri bought Chevy his first pet. Terri and I went away to New Orleans to "The Essence Festival" on our first couples trip together, and we met up with Sandy. That was one of my best trips—we partied all night long and didn't go back to the hotel until 8:00 a.m. the next morning.

However, for some reason, I woke up saying to myself, "I don't want to put another dress on." Do not ask me where that came from—just like I didn't know where the attraction toward Terri came from. The following week, I had a job interview with the Baltimore City Police Department, and I wore a dress for my interview. I also brought a pair of pants and a blouse with me and decided to replace the dress with my pants and blouse after feeling uncomfortable. I felt free, and from that day forward, I changed my entire wardrobe to men's clothing.

Terri was very inspirational in my life. When I would try to talk myself out of going back to school to obtain my degree, she would give me that push by encouraging me to further my education. Thanks to her, I attended Catonsville Community College and obtained my Associate's Degree in Human Services Mental Health.

Terri is the reason today that I am an addiction counselor

—because of her encouragement. I always had the natural ability to assist others. Since I was a kid, I would protect other kids in school if I felt they were being bullied. I was "the mascot" of my family, trying to interject through tension, anger, conflict, violence, or other unpleasant situations within the family. I have always been protective over my mom, ensuring that her siblings or anyone else would not bother her. I also witnessed drug addiction in my family and in the neighborhood of Cherry Hill; in other words, I was fully aware of my new career path. I pursued that path and am still working as an addiction counselor today.

Terri and I had a peaceful relationship without any drama —until one day I caught her with her husband. That did not go too well at all, but she stated that it wouldn't happen again. However, I realized that Terri was not ready to be in a relationship, and our relationship ended in November of 1996.

6

LOVE, LOSS, AND RESILIENCE

In December 1996, I met Petra, a hair stylist, at the Pagan Best Salon. Well, I actually met Petra the first time in 1989 at Vigg Hair and Beauty, and we were both pregnant—I was pregnant with my daughter, Ray, and she was pregnant with her son, Tye. However, when I met up with Petra at Pagan, she did not appear to be her jolly self as she was when I met her previously at Vigg Hair and Beauty.

Toni was my hair stylist, and one day I asked her what was up with Petra. I wanted to know if she was still married. Toni stated,

"She's ok."

I told Toni that I liked Petra and thought she was cute. Once I came from under the dryer, I started talking a little trash to Petra, and she started talking trash back. Petra threw me off guard because I was not expecting her to come at me like that. I asked Petra if she would like to go out with me for a drink at Pargos Restaurant once she got off from work. She stated, "Yes."

Petra was a feisty woman—slightly shorter than I am, with brown skin and pretty features. Petra was my type of woman because she had the qualities that I like in a woman, such as her beauty and her height. I can say that in this relationship, we met each other's needs. However, I must say that at times we overly met each other's needs due to the conflict it could bring when we didn't.

Petra and my relationship grew deeper, and she and her three children moved in with my two children and me. That was a busy house! Can you imagine five kids in a two-bedroom apartment? There were days that seemed to demand more energy than I had to give, and there were days that went smoothly. Some days they would be loud and bicker over who got to play with a toy first, etc.

Petra had a daughter, Tic, and two sons, Tye and Xva. Overall, the children got along very well, and it was good that they came along—because that was when I started letting my children go outside to play. My children were more homebodies; they enjoyed being home and still do today.

Petra and I had many adventurous trips with the children, but I tell you, there were plenty of difficulties. There were many traumatic situations and challenges that Petra and her kids endured during her previous marriage; however, I prefer not to elaborate on those traumatic experiences.

Petra and I had a beautiful relationship in the beginning. We loved to dance and went to many gay affairs—both of us loved to throw down on the dance floor. We also enjoyed watching the Ravens and loved our kicker, Matt Stover. When Stover would kick a field goal, Petra and I would stand up and shout, "Stoverrrr!"

We had our union on June 9, 2001, although same-sex marriage was not legalized at that time. During the preparation for the union, I started feeling that I wanted to back out because of the many conflicts Petra and I had experienced. I went through with the union, thinking that things might get better since we were going to be married. Petra did all the decorations at the American Legion Hall, and it was set up beautifully. I tell you, we partied—all night long, with Petra and I barely sitting down to eat. We were always in rhythm with each other and could dance all night long together. My love for Petra grew stronger once we had the union. I can say that we had our good times and our bad times; however, I was still praying that things would be better.

I feel one of the biggest mistakes I made in this relationship was when I finished school at Catonsville Community College and thought I could fix Petra and her children's problems. I have my degree in Human Services Mental Health, so I thought, "Oh, I can help them." I learned in school that you should never try to counsel any family members or your spouse. Petra still says today, "You saved my life because if it wasn't for you I don't know where I would be." I am happy that she received some of the help she needed. However, I can tell you I was mentally drained from everything that came with Petra's situation.

I always knew that Petra was extremely jealous, and today I can admit that I played a part in that. I always had a thing that no matter what, I was going to still be friends with my exes—which was not good for Petra. In retrospect, I believe I went to the extreme. Each one of my exes hung out with us every now and then. Petra did eventually become close to Jane, and she even participated in the union. I had the nerve to wonder why Petra would yell at me! I really did not see a problem with being friends with exes, although Petra used to get upset about it. Petra already had insecurities about herself, and this made things worse.

I know you are probably thinking, "Really? You didn't realize it was unhealthy to continue a friendship with your ex and expect the person you are in a relationship with to associate with your ex, as well?!" No, I really did not realize the effect that my exes had on our relationship.

As time progressed, the relationship between Petra and me diminished due to constant arguing and, on many occasions, physical fights. I wasn't used to this type of behavior, and it wasn't something I wanted to adapt to. My love for Petra became so unhealthy that I lost my sense of identity, as everything in my life began to revolve around her and our relationship.. Everything in my life revolved around that one person. This is one of the worst things you can do to yourself —because when that person is gone, all you have is yourself. Then what!!!

In turn, this was one of the causes of my struggle with the near-end of our relationship. I think I focused so much on trying to make Petra happy that I forgot the importance of my own happiness. One thing I know I didn't lose focus on was my children, thanks to God. However, I have learned a lot from that relationship and apply those lessons today. If you met me now (single, 100% in control of my own life, bossing my career, and completely in love with the lifestyle I've since created for myself), you would never believe that I gave up my entire identity for a woman.

Petra and my relationship officially ended on September 8, 2005. When we were no longer intimate, I knew something was wrong, and our relationship became unpredictable. I tell you—this was another one of the most difficult breakups I had to experience. As I worked through the pain of my relationship with Petra, I reached a breaking point—I knew I couldn't carry the weight of all this drama anymore. I was emotionally drained and spiritually exhausted.

One day, as I sat reflecting on everything, Mary J. Blige's song "No More Drama" came on. When she sang, "I'm so tired of all this drama. No more pain, no more pain," it was as if she were speaking directly to me. Every word pierced my soul. That song became my anthem—it reminded me that I deserved peace. God was lifting me from all the hurt and emotional baggage I had been holding onto. I knew in that moment that it was time to move on, to truly let go of the pain, and to step into the peace that God had waiting for me.

I sat with myself for eight long years after that—not because I wanted to, but because God sat me down to heal. This was the first time in my life without a boyfriend or girlfriend. See, this was unusual for me because my two relationships before Petra were back-to-back. I have been in relationships since I was 13 years old, so this was the first time I had ever sat with myself. I must say it was tough in the beginning, but God knew what I needed. I thank Him today for that time I sat with myself because I did a lot of work on me.

I received mental health services and was diagnosed with Major Depressive Disorder. Then God brought Joyce Myers into my life, and I read the book "Self Matters" by Dr. Phil. After that, I read the entire Bible and wrote about what I learned in the Old Testament.

Watching and listening to Dr. Phil motivated me to do some serious work on myself. I also turned to the Bible and reflected on how Job overcame so many obstacles in his life. I said to myself,

"I'm sitting here crying over a relationship, and I'm reading about all that Job had to overcome by losing his family."

I told myself I needed to come out of this rut—and I tell you, my dog CJ was right there with me the entire time.

I allowed the children to live with Levi during the week because they kept complaining about their school at Kenwood High. They wanted to return to Carver Vocational

High School, where they had attended before we moved to Middle River. In the end, it worked out for the best—not only did they get to be where they felt comfortable, but it also spared them from witnessing my personal struggles.

Dr. Phil's teachings helped me gain a better understanding of the "Authentic Self" and how I had to leave the "Fictional Self" behind. God helped me overcome it all when I began to have a closer relationship with Him. I joined the Church of Christ Eastside, and I tell you, God was doing some work on me. Another inspirational person in my life is CeCe Winans —she is my favorite gospel singer. Her music has always been a source of comfort and strength for me.

One year, I had the privilege of seeing CeCe Winans live in concert at the Lyric Theater in Baltimore. I was sitting just three seats from the stage, completely in awe. As the concert was coming to an end, I couldn't believe she was about to leave without singing my favorite song—"Alabaster Box."

Without thinking, I stood up and called out to her,

"I know you are not going to leave without singing 'Alabaster Box'!"

CeCe paused, glanced at one of her background singers, shrugged her shoulders, and said,

"I guess we have to sing it."

And let me tell you—they sang that song, right there! The spirit in the room was incredible, and everyone felt it. When the show was over, people kept coming up to me, thanking me for speaking up. They were just as moved as I was. It was a moment I will never forget.

The struggle I experienced at that time was necessary because it helped me see that I don't need anything or anyone to define who Candy is— all I need is God! I continue to face many struggles—that's just life. However, I am determined never to let anyone bring me down like that again! If you knew me back then and saw who I am today, you wouldn't believe the transformation. God led me to do some incredible work on myself, hear!

During the eight years I spent reflecting and growing, I completely revamped my wardrobe, returning to women's clothing.

7

REFLECTIONS ON LEGACY AND HOPE

In February 2013, my best friend Doris told me she saw Marlo on Facebook, and I decided to reach out. Marlo and I grew up together, and our mothers were best friends. We hadn't seen each other in 30 years, and reconnecting felt like fate. Marlo, whom I lovingly called my African Queen, was dark-skinned, pretty with beautiful white teeth, and a little taller than me. She was also resilient, guarded, and very discreet—a total contrast to my go-with-the-flow, free-spirited personality. Despite our differences, we began a relationship. While we created beautiful memories traveling to places like Canada, San Diego, and Las Vegas, our connection struggled due to our differences and Marlo's discomfort with openly acknowledging our relationship. I have to give Marlo her credit, though—she did say that she was not ready for a relationship at the time we hooked up, but I was adamant about us being together.

This relationship taught me an important lesson: if someone says they're not ready for a relationship, believe them. You cannot force someone to give you their whole self.

I also learned the importance of never compromising my identity for the sake of a relationship.

One decision I still regret while dealing with Marlo was removing my son Chevy's videos from YouTube. Chevy used to record me without my awareness. The videos featured various things I did that made him laugh, so he decided to post them on YouTube. Chevy would hide on the floor or on the steps where I couldn't see him. One video showed my dog, CJ, and me arguing. CJ called himself fussing back at me when I caught him peeing in the house, and he actually would bark back at me. Marlo insisted that I take them down, but in hindsight, I shouldn't have allowed someone to have that much control over me. She gave me an ultimatum: either have the videos taken down or we couldn't be together. In other words, it could ruin her reputation to be with someone who had these types of videos on social media.

I had Chevy remove the videos, but all Marlo did was find something else about me that she wanted to change. The relationship became, "Damn if I do, and damn if I don't!" I am still disappointed in myself today for making that type of sacrifice. I actually allowed someone to have that much power over me in order for our relationship to continue. However, Chevy was able to reload some of the videos— thank God, now I can still watch my CJ. Chevy surprised me for my 53rd birthday with the videos.

Marlo and my relationship officially ended on October 9, 2016.

I am still very grateful that Marlo came back into my life and that I had the chance to have a relationship with her. Marlo was another great influence in my life and pushed me to better myself. She encouraged me to return to school and was there for me during one of the scarier times in my life.

In February 2016, I was diagnosed with uterine cancer.

Thanks to my meticulous tracking of my menstrual cycle, I caught it early. My sister-in-law, Lisa, had taught me to keep a monthly schedule when I was 13, and that habit helped save my life. At the time, I was attending Coppin State University, working toward my bachelor's degree in Social Work. On February 25, 2016, during a semester filled with challenges, I received the life-changing news from Dr. Marly while sitting in class. I know you're probably thinking, "Of all places to receive that information," but being surrounded by my teacher and classmates turned out to be a blessing. They immediately prayed over me and offered their unwavering support, which gave me strength in that moment.

Despite the diagnosis, I remained determined to push forward. Marlo stood by me every step of the way, offering constant care and encouragement. Through surgery and recovery, I continued my studies and earned all "A's" that semester. On February 12, 2017, I received the 2nd Chance Award in recognition of my perseverance, as well as an award for the highest GPA in Social Work. Finally, in 2018, I graduated with my bachelor's degree in Social Work—a testament to resilience and the power of faith.

This experience reinforced the importance of listening to your body and never ignoring what it's trying to tell you. It's a reminder for everyone to prioritize regular checkups—such as Pap smears, mammograms, and prostate exams for men. Catching something early can make all the difference; well, it certainly did for me.

In 2016, I celebrated my 50th birthday surrounded by loved ones. It was a night to remember—filled with laughter, dancing, and gratitude. Marlo and Petra worked together to create a beautiful event, decorating the space and ensuring every detail reflected the joy of my special day. My brother

Daven and his friend Quin played the music, setting the perfect tone for an unforgettable night.

I danced all night long, and of course, I had my special dance with my mommy. We threw down! Quin and I brought the house down with "Hotline Bling" by Drake. My family and friends always know how to turn it up when we have a party—here! Once I hear music, I can't stop my body from moving and hitting a beat—I just love to dance. One of my colleagues even calls me "Thunder" because I never miss a rhythm, and my old director lovingly named me the "Dancing Queen." Even at work, if a colleague starts hitting a beat on the desk, I roll right with it.

That night wasn't just a party—it was a testament to the love and support I've been blessed with throughout my life. Family has always been the heart of my life. My children, Chevy and Ray, and my grandson, Lan, bring immeasurable joy to my journey.

Each of my relationships taught me valuable lessons. Levi gave me unconditional love and our beautiful children. Terri showed me the courage to explore my identity. Petra offered companionship and the experience of union, and Marlo encouraged me to better myself and cared for me during one of the most challenging times of my life.

Like when I had the goal of becoming an author—and I began writing my book in 2007, but I only completed about 30 pages because I wasn't as focused as I needed to be—until Marlo introduced me to her best friend, Angel. Angel is my girl, and I am so happy that Marlo brought her into my life.

One day, I was talking to Marlo and Angel, and they said to me,

"When are you going to finish your book?"

Then, they had the nerve to say,

"You can't say you are focusing on school because you finished school."

I replied,

"Y'all right. I am going to work on it now while I have the opportunity."

That was one of the best suggestions they could have made in that moment, because I completed my book. Through the process of writing, I learned to welcome change—and anyone who knows me would tell you change was difficult for me. I realized that writing my book was not only closure for the first part of my life, but it was also therapy for me. I feel so complete, and I have learned that completeness does not have to come from having a relationship with someone—it comes from God and within. I do not ever remember feeling like this.

I remember saying to myself,

"I'm going to stop giving permanent space to temporary things. I'm going to stop giving my future to the past, and I'm going to stop focusing on things that have faded."

Now, you know I couldn't leave out my babies—Chevy, Ray, and Lan. We share a bond that is truly unbreakable, and I thank God every day for blessing Levi and me with such wonderful children.

My grandson, Lan, is 12 years old and means the world to me. I haven't seen a child like him—he is a true blessing from God. Lan excels in school and has big dreams of becoming a professional football player. His team, the Stembridge Colts, recently won the Championship for the Upper Chesapeake Youth Football League. Lan was awarded Defensive Player of the Championship and even crowned Homecoming King for his football team.

On top of that, Lan told me he's ready to get baptized because he wants God to forgive him for his sins. I couldn't imagine what sins he was talking about, but I didn't ask—I just said, "Okay." He was baptized at my church on June 2, 2024. I am so proud of him and excited to see the amazing things God has in store for his future.

My daughter, Ray, is a wonderful mother, and my son, Chevy, is a fantastic uncle. Ray completed her Master's Degree in Cybersecurity with an Organizational Resilience specialization, while Chevy has become an accomplished author. I'm so proud of both of them for their hard work and dedication.

Family is everything to me, and Chevy, Ray, and I make it a priority to stay connected. Every night, we get on three-way calls—it's a must. Some weekends, I let them slide and talk to them individually, but most nights you can find us laughing and catching up together. I'm not the best with technology, but I've learned how to do three-way calls and even DUO calls! Still, we prefer three-way conversations.

"Ma, it's already been forty minutes," Chevy will say.

"Oh, I guess you've had enough," I reply, and we all crack up laughing. Chevy loves how Ray nonchalantly says, "Ma, what are you talking about, huhhh?" He finds it hilarious—and honestly, she is funny.

My kids love to tease me, and we laugh the entire time on the phone. Chevy's friend Kyle often joins in and chimes in on our conversations. Kyle is like one of my baby boys too—if I call you baby boy or baby girl, that means I really care about you.

Now, let me tell you about that grandson of mine. Lan is a piece of work! On some weekends, he comes over to stay with me, and we have our special time together. We lie under each other and watch our favorite shows—"American Ninja Warrior," Ravens football games, and cooking shows.

Lan and I also have this little thing we call "sniff sniff." He'll say,

"Mama, it's time for us to sniff sniff,"

and I'll sniff my pillow while he sniffs his blanket. Then, he'll tell me it's time to switch, so we'll sniff each other's pillow and blanket. It might sound silly, but it's our special bond. The pillow is meaningful to me because I used to suck my thumb and always had a security pillow. Lan has the same trait—he needs his security blanket. It's amazing to see how something like that carries over through generations.

These little moments with my children and grandson remind me of how blessed I am. Whether it's sharing laughs on the phone or creating memories with Lan during his visits, I cherish every single one.

My journey has always been deeply rooted in faith, and God has placed incredible tools and people in my life to help me navigate challenges.

One day, I received this message from my pastor at Morning Star Baptist Church:

"Everyone that happens to be wounded, there is a miracle that needs to be talked about."

I myself am a walking miracle. I have been through a lot, and I survived my wounds. I will never be afraid to win because I saw God win every time. God still has me standing because I placed my trust in Him.

Second, God brought Joyce Meyer into my life. She helped me understand how God works in our lives and why we all experience trials and tribulations. Joyce says,

"Many of the tests and trials we encounter are intended to help build our faith. Faith only grows as we use it. The more we use it, the stronger it gets. God is good, and He has a good plan for our lives."

Every year, my son Chevy buys me Joyce Meyer's "365

Devotions to Start Your Day Right." I also receive her yearly calendar. Joyce's "365 Devotions" inspires me every day and helps me start my day with God, setting the tone for everything I do.

Dr. Phil McGraw has also played a significant role in my journey. His teachings helped me understand the importance of accountability and boundaries. His wisdom reminds me to focus on what I can control and let go of what I can't. By following these lessons, I've grown stronger emotionally and mentally.

Today, I am grounded in self-love and faith. I've learned to put myself first, set boundaries, and let God guide my path. As Marvin Sapp sings, "I'm stronger, wiser, and better." I now embrace change and view it as an opportunity for growth.

Part of my journey has been finding fulfillment in my career. I have a Bachelor's Degree in Social Work, but when the pandemic hit in 2017, I made the decision to continue working as an addictions counselor. For over 20 years, I have been helping young adults, adults, and the elderly address and overcome their addictions. Despite the challenges, I still enjoy helping people on their path to recovery—it's incredibly rewarding to make a difference in the lives of others.

As I move forward, I hold on to the lessons I've learned, the love of my family, and my unwavering faith in God's plan. I trust that He will continue to guide me as I strive to live authentically and help others do the same.

This chapter of my life is closed, but I carry the lessons with me as I move into the future. Writing this book has been therapeutic, giving me closure and a renewed sense of purpose. I am excited for the next phase of my journey and trust that God has incredible plans ahead.

"Saul was my very first stylist. My big brother dressed me for my kindergarten picture."

ACKNOWLEDGMENTS

This memoir is a testament to the love and support I have received throughout my journey. I want to thank my family, especially my siblings Saul, Nelly, and Dave, for being my lifelong anchors. To my sister-in-law Lisa, whose wisdom and encouragement taught me the importance of knowing my body and facing challenges with strength, I am forever grateful.

To my mother, Joyce, the greatest woman I know. Your phenomenal spirit and unwavering love have shaped me into who I am today. You are my rock, my light, and my inspiration, and I will always cherish the bond we share.

To my mother's husband, Lance—thank you for being such a wonderful husband to my mother. I am truly grateful that she found the man of her dreams—someone who loves and cherishes her the way she deserves.

To my godmother Lauren, you've always been an incredible influence in my life. You hold a very special place in my heart. Thank you for always watching over me.

To my nieces, nephews, great-nieces, and great-nephews, I am so proud of each of you. You are truly the Bomb.com! Seeing you all become wonderful parents and exceptional individuals fills my heart with pride.

To my children, Chevy and Ray, and my grandson Lan, you are my greatest blessings. Chevy, your creativity as an author inspires me every day. Ray, your dedication to achieving your Master's Degree has shown me what determination can achieve. Lan, you are a shining star. Your excellence in school, achievements, and kind heart remind me of God's incredible work.

I also want to acknowledge my best friend Doris, whose loyalty and encouragement have been a constant in my life. To my dear friends and extended family, thank you for your unwavering support and for bringing so much joy to my journey.

To Levi, for teaching me love and patience. To Terri, for helping me discover the courage to explore my identity. To Petra, for sharing in the experience of union. And to Marlo, for being a source of care during some of my most challenging times. Each of you has played a significant role in my growth, and I honor the lessons you've taught me.

To my new dog Theo—another soul I appreciate in my life who truly loves me. You are my person, and yes, I said person!

Lastly, to the Cherry Hill community, where my roots were planted, and to every person who has touched my life in a meaningful way—this book would not exist without your love and encouragement.

www.ingramcontent.com/pod-product-compliance
Lightning Source LLC
Chambersburg PA
CBHW051234120626
46547CB00013B/1634